The Cycle of a Dream

A Kid's Introduction to Structural Racism in America

by Kimberly Narain, MD, PhD, MPH

Illustrations by Mike Motz

To Abri and Eli,
who inspire me to fight
to make the world
a little better every day.

I want to sincerely thank the following reviewers
for helping my vision take shape:
Thomas Cauley, BS; Daniel Kozman, MD, MPH;
Mahmud Narain, MBA; Joan Reede, MD, MPH, MS, MBA;
Kafayat Tijani, M.Ed and Ashaunta Tumblin Anderson, MD, MPH, MSHS

The Long Nightmare: Slavery in America

In 1619, some people from the African country of Angola were kidnapped by people from Europe and sold to English settlers living in Virginia. A "settler" is a person who moves with other people to live in a new country. The settlers treated the African people like property instead of human beings. The settlers would beat the African people to get them to work for long hours with no pay. Treating human beings like property is called "slavery," and people living in slavery are called "slaves."

In 1662, a court decided that children born to slaves were the property of the "slave master," the mother's owner. This decision gave slave masters the power to sell the children of slaves and break up African families. This decision also guaranteed that generations of African people would never have freedom.

Nearly 400,000 African people were kidnapped and brought to America between 1619 and 1807. Many slaves worked on farms called "plantations," picking crops like tobacco, sugar, and cotton, which the plantation owners sold for money. Since the plantation owners did not have to pay slaves for their work, they started getting very rich.

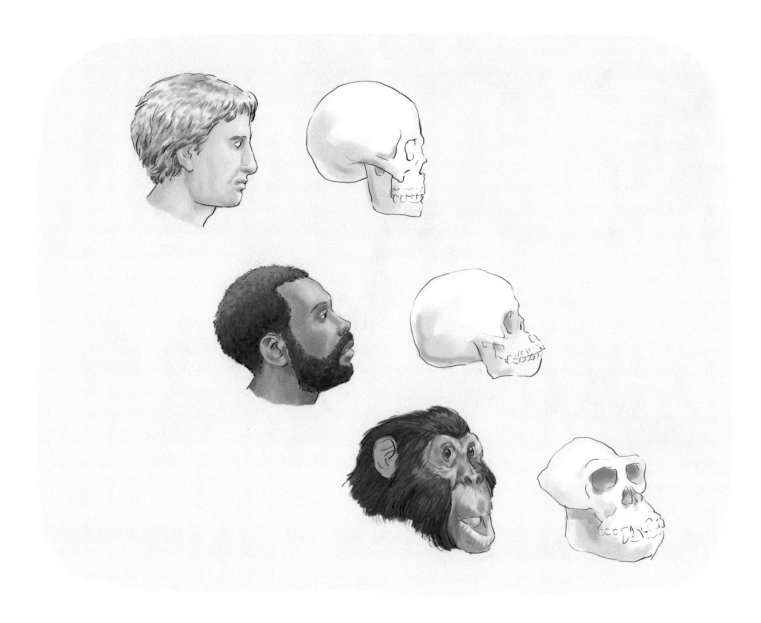

People who were getting rich off slavery did not want it to end, so they told lies about the African people to make everyone feel like slavery was a good thing. They made up stories that people with ancestors from Africa, "Black people," were different and worse than people with ancestors from Europe, "White people." They said Black people were more like animals than humans, that they were stupid, lazy, violent criminals, and liked slavery.

Racism is the belief that people can be put into groups based on how they look, and that some groups of people, or races, are better than others. Racist ideas were spread through science and art. The first plays ever created by people in America were called "Minstrel Shows" and had White actors who painted their faces black pretending to be silly, lazy, stupid, or happy slaves. Racism made many White people feel like it was fine to keep Black people in slavery.

Rules were made to stop Black people from learning so that it would be more difficult for them to fight against slavery. "Slave patrols" were groups of White people who were in charge of searching the homes of slaves to make sure they were not learning how to read or write.

As more people living in the northern states of America created businesses that did not need slaves to make money, some White people began criticizing slavery. Some northern states began to pass laws making slavery illegal. Some Black people, like Harriet Tubman, escaped to freedom in northern states and helped others to do the same. Other Black people, like Frederick Douglass and Booker T. Washington, learned to read and write even though it was against the law. They started writing and speaking out about the cruelty of slavery. People who worked to end slavery were called "abolitionists."

Since many people in southern states were still making money off of slavery, they did not want it to end. Eleven southern states created their own country called the Confederate States of America where slavery was still legal. But many people in the northern states wanted to keep the southern and northern states together in one country, which led to the Civil War in 1861.

The soldiers in the northern states thought that they would easily defeat the soldiers in the southern states, but that did not happen. After a year of war, President Abraham Lincoln declared that all slaves in the southern states were free in the Emancipation Proclamation. Without slaves, many southern states had a hard time making enough money to keep fighting the war. In 1865, the Confederate army surrendered, bringing southern and northern states back together into one country.

A Dream Turns into a New Nightmare: Life after Slavery

On June 19, 1865, in Texas, almost 3 years after the Emancipation Proclamation, the last slaves found out that they were free. New laws made the nearly 4 million newly freed Black people now "citizens" of America who had rights that should be protected. For the first time, it seemed like the "American Dream," the ability to achieve success if you work hard, would be available to Black people.

In 1870, Black men were given the right to vote in elections. Voting in elections had the potential to give Black men a voice in deciding which people would make decisions about what laws were created and how money was spent in the towns where they lived, in their state, and in the entire country. Black men quickly started voting, and some black men even became law makers, but the opportunity for Black people to succeed in America as White people had did not last long.

Many states found new ways to treat Black people unfairly. The unfair treatment of different groups of people is called "discrimination." Some White people in the southern states did not want Black people to have any power to make choices about how they lived, and they did not want to have to pay them much money to work, so they made laws called the "Black Codes." The Black Codes forced Black people to work for White people for very little pay, and also made it really hard for them to vote in elections.

The Black Code laws said that people have to own land, pay money, and pass a reading test to vote. Since Black people could not own land as slaves and were not allowed to learn to read or write, it was tough for them to meet this voting rule. Groups like the Ku Klux Klan also used threats and violence to try to make Black people too scared to vote. While some Black people were still able to vote, many were blocked from doing this.

Blocking most Black people in the southern states from voting left White people in charge of deciding which neighborhoods had safe places to live, which ones had places to work and shop, which ones had places for sick people to get help, and which ones had enough money for schools.

Many states in the south also made laws that forced Black people to live in different neighborhoods, work in different jobs, go to different schools, see different doctors, and even use different doors and bathrooms than White people. If Black people did not follow these rules, the police could put them in jail. Forcing Black and White people to be away from each other in every area of life is called "segregation."

Blacks in southern states did make their own neighborhoods with businesses, schools, and churches, but White people usually lived in neighborhoods with safer homes, more places to work and shop, and better supplies for schools. Sometimes if the Black neighborhoods were doing very well, some White people would get angry and burn the neighborhood down. In some cases, White people would force Black people off of their land and take it for themselves.

States in the northern part of America that did not have this segregation had other ways to keep Black and White people separate. When Black people tried to buy homes in neighborhoods where White people lived, most banks would not lend them the money because they were afraid Black people would destroy the neighborhoods. They also made rules that kept White people from selling their homes to Black people. When Black people figured out a way to get a loan from a bank, the bank made them pay more than White people had to pay when buying the same type of home.

A few Black people started to buy homes where White people lived and the White people got scared that their neighborhood would become filled with crime, so they sold their homes and moved to different neighborhoods. When White people move away from an area once people from different racial groups move in, this is called "white flight."

When "white flight" happened, the people in charge of deciding which neighborhoods got money would usually give less money to the neighborhood than before, and eventually the homes in these neighborhoods would get damaged, most places to work and shop would leave, the schools would lose money, and the houses would be worth less money. When other Black people would try to buy homes in these neighborhoods, the banks often would not lend them the money because they thought the neighborhoods were too dangerous, which led to these neighborhoods losing even more money. "Redlining" is refusing to give services to people who live in areas where there is a high number of people who are not White.

Black people in the northern states also had more trouble finding jobs than White people with the same or less skills. They were also paid less money than White people for doing the same types of jobs.

By the 1950s, Black people were getting very tired of being treated unfairly. Black leaders like Malcolm X spoke out about the damage discrimination and segregation were doing to Black people. Martin Luther King, Jr. shared his hope for a country where Black people would be judged on who they were and not the color of their skin in his "I Have a Dream" speech.

Many people of different races started coming together to "protest," or show that they disagreed with discrimination and segregation. They protested by marching, breaking the laws of segregation, and refusing to buy things from places that discriminated against Black people. "Boycotting" is refusing to make deals with someone or buy anything from them as a form of protest. People who protested were sometimes beaten, put in jail, and even killed.

Huey P. Newton and Bobby Seale formed the Black Panther Party to fight against unfair treatment of Black people and to give things that many Black people needed like food and treatment when they were sick. Some White people were afraid that groups like the Black Panther Party were having too much influence on Black people, so the leaders of the Federal Bureau of Investigation (FBI), the group in America in charge of deciding who the most dangerous people are, made plans to destroy the Black Panther Party.

A Dream Deferred: Life after Civil Rights

After many years of protest and the making of new laws, segregation and discrimination finally became illegal by the end of the 1960s. These laws allowed people from countries all over the world to come to America. The end of legal segregation and discrimination led many people to believe that after nearly 350 years of unequal treatment in America, Black people would finally have the same opportunities as White people. There was hope that more Black people would get jobs that paid enough money for them to buy the things they needed. There was also hope that Black people would finally have the chance to live in neighborhoods with safe homes, plenty of places to work, nice places to shop, places to go when they were sick, and schools that had enough money for the students.

Although segregation and discrimination were no longer legal in America after 1968, once again new plans and laws were made to deny Black people access to the American Dream. The police spent more time looking for people doing crimes in neighborhoods where Black people lived than they did in neighborhoods where White people lived. Because the police spent more time looking for crime in neighborhoods where Black people lived, they arrested more Black people than White people. The police continued treating Black people worse than they treated White people, even if the Black people were not doing any crime at all. If a police officer hurt a Black person very badly, they were usually not punished.

Laws were also made that led to much tougher punishments for Black people than White people for doing the same types of crimes. This discrimination increased the number of Black people that went to jail, especially Black men. Many Black people lost family members, children lost time with their fathers, and families lost money. Once people got out of jail, they had an even harder time finding a job than they did before. Many had trouble finding a place to live or getting food to eat. Many lost the ability to get care if they were sick. And all of these people lost their right to vote in elections.

It's Time to Wake Up

Even though slavery ended more than 150 years ago, slavery and the racism that was used to keep it going still harms Black people today. The same money that was stolen from Black people by forcing them to work for free was used by people who owned slaves to buy homes, build schools, and create businesses that continue to make money for their family members who are alive today. For another 100 years Black people were not allowed to attend the schools, work in the businesses, and live in the neighborhoods that were often built by the money made from their work. Because of segregation and discrimination, most Black people still live in neighborhoods where there are fewer places to get help if you are sick, where there are fewer places to work, shop, or play, and where the schools get less money. Growing up in and living in these types of neighborhoods makes it hard for some Black people to get a good education, get a nice job, start a business, stay healthy, and pass money down to their family members. For every $1 a typical Black family has, a typical White family has $10.

Segregation and discrimination are barriers that make it more challenging for Black people to achieve the American Dream. Because many people in America do not learn about the barriers Black people deal with in this country and the history of those barriers, some still believe that Black people are stupid, lazy, criminal, and dangerous. These damaging beliefs about Black people are often made stronger by what is seen in movies, on television shows, and in the news. These false beliefs often impact how Black people are treated. For example, the belief that Black people are dangerous criminals sometimes leads people to be afraid of Black people who are not doing anything wrong.

Making the Dream Reality

People from all different backgrounds and racial groups have worked together to bring America closer to equal opportunity for everyone in the past. Now more than ever, people need to continue to work together to help make the American Dream a reality for everyone. Here are a few ways to help make opportunity more equal for all people:

• Learn more about the history and experiences of groups of people that are different from your own.

• Think about how you may have treated someone unfairly based on how they look, what religion they are, what language they speak, or where they are from.

• Speak up when you see unfair treatment of someone based on how they look, what religion they are, what language they speak, or where they are from.

• Look for ways to use your skills and talents to increase opportunities for people that experience discrimination.

• Support people, businesses, and groups that share your belief in equality of opportunity for everyone.

Meet
Kimberly Narain, MD, PhD, MPH

Motivated by her own battle with chronic disease, Dr. Kimberly Narain has devoted her career to ensuring everyone has the opportunity to be healthy. She is a wife, a mother, an internal medicine physician, and a researcher focused on improving the health of underserved and underresourced populations.

CPSIA information can be obtained
at www.ICGtesting.com
Printed in the USA
LVHW072020191120
672184LV00019B/370

9 781087 903088